Joke Books

by Erika L. Shores

Consulting Editor: Gail Saunders-Smith, PhD

CAPSTONE PRESS
a capstone imprint

Pebble Books are published by Capstone Press,
1710 Roe Crest Drive, North Mankato, Minnesota 56003.
www.capstonepub.com

Library of Congress Cataloging-in-Publication Data
Shores, Erika L., 1976–
  Silly classroom jokes / by Erika L. Shores.
    p. cm. — (Pebble books. Joke books)
  Includes bibliographical references.
  Summary: "Simple text and color photographs present classroom jokes"—
Provided by publisher.
  ISBN 978-1-4296-7563-5 (library binding)
  1. Schools—Juvenile humor. 2. Wit and humor, Juvenile. I. Title. II. Series.
  PN6231.S3S89 2012
  818'.602—dc23   2011030105

Editorial Credits
Gillia Olson, editor; Gene Bentdahl, designer; Sarah Schuette, studio specialist;
  Marcy Morin, studio scheduler; Kathy McColley, production specialist

Photo Credits
All photos by Capstone Studio/Karon Dubke

Note to Parents and Teachers

The Pebble Jokes set supports English language arts standards related
to reading a wide range of print for personal fulfillment. Early readers
may need assistance to read some of the words and to use the Table of
Contents, Read More, and Internet Sites sections of this book.

Printed in the United States of America in Stevens Point, Wisconsin.
082013   007656R

Table of Contents

Why did the dog do so well in school?

Because it was the teacher's pet.

What is more amazing than a talking dog?

A spelling bee.

What did the spelling teacher say to the student who fell down?

R-U-O-K?

What happened when the teacher tied all the students' shoelaces together?

They had a class trip!

Why did the girl eat her math test?

Her teacher said it was a piece of cake.

What did the teacher do with the cheese's test?

He grated it.

Why did the computer squeak?

Someone stepped on the mouse!

Why was the clock itching?

Because it had ticks.

Why did the computer get glasses?

To improve its web sight.

Why did the computer sneeze?

It had a virus.

What did the astronaut's mother give her for school?

Launch money.

What do astronauts get on their homework?

Gold stars.

Why did the clock get in trouble?

It tocked too much in class.

Why did the egg get thrown out of class?

It kept telling yokes.

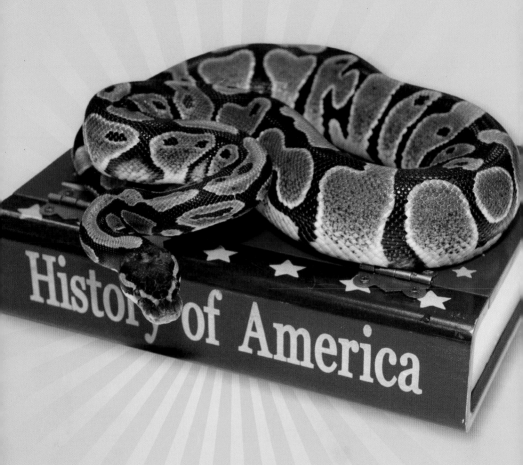

What is a snake's favorite subject?

Hissstory.

Why was the snake late for school?

It hissed the bus.

What happens if you take the school bus home?

The police will make you bring it back.

What did the bus driver say to the fish?

"What school do you go to?"

What do elves learn
in school?

The elf-abet.

What do elves do
after school?

Gnomework.

Read More

Connolly, Sean, and Kay Barnham. *The School's Cool Joke Book.* Laugh Out Loud. New York: Windmill Books, 2012.

Dahl, Michael. *Chuckle Squad: Jokes about Classrooms, Sports, Food, Teachers, and Other School Subjects.* Michael Dahl Presents Super Funny Joke Books. Mankato, Minn.: Picture Window Books, 2011.

Rosenbloom, Joseph. *School Jokes.* Giggle Fit. New York: Sterling Publishing Co., 2004.

Internet Sites

FactHound offers a safe, fun way to find Internet sites related to this book. All of the sites on FactHound have been researched by our staff.

Here's all you do:

Visit *www.facthound.com*

Type in this code: 9781429675635

Super-cool stuff! Check out projects, games and lots more at
www.capstonekids.com

Word Count: 234 **Grade:** 1
Early-Intervention Level: 18